Deceive the Dragon

Negotiating to retain power

Deceive the Dragon

Negotiating to retain power

Leonie McKeon

DoctorZed
Publishing
www.doctorzed.com

Books may be ordered through booksellers or by contacting:
www.leoniemckeon.com

ISBN: 978-0-6481314-2-7 (hc)
ISBN: 978-0-6481314-4-1 (sc)
ISBN: 978-0-6481314-3-4 (ebk)

A CiP number for this title can be found at the National Library of Australia.

Cover image © Trish Pollock

Printed in Australia, UK and USA.
rev. date 28/06/2018

Contents

Acknowledgements

*A*s I continue to write *The Dao of Negotiation*, I realise more and more the rich subtleties that distinguish one strategy from another, and how multiple strategies can be simultaneously at play. As anyone who has engaged in a complex project like writing a book will know, it is crucial to have someone to bounce ideas off. It has been a pleasure to work with Organisational Psychologist Shelley Rogers, who assisted me in thinking through some of the examples. Shelley has had her own experiences of China, which has made her insights valuable. I would also like to thank Jennifer McKeon who continues to read and re-read the drafts and has provided much needed support and belief in the project. Finally, many thanks to Cassandra Heffernan for her wonderful research skills, and to everyone else behind the scenes who has made *Deceive the Dragon* possible.

"Therefore, just as water retains no constant shape, so in warfare there are no constant conditions."
Sun Tzu, *The Art of War*

Leonie's Journey Continues

*A*fter being advised to go to Taiwan by an English guy, my travelling companion and I met at the youth hostel in Hong Kong, we arrived in Taipei, Taiwan, with limited money. The piece of information we were not told was that if you wanted to teach English in Taiwan you had to speak with an American accent. We discovered this after reading several noticeboards in the hostel we were staying at in Taipei. Of course these were the days of no internet – yes a world without the internet – so we relied on pieces of paper pinned to noticeboards for information about employment, accommodation and things for sale. The notices with advertisements for English teachers all said 'American English teacher wanted'. You did not need a teaching background, nor were you required to speak Mandarin Chinese; you just needed to speak English with an American accent. I was aware that in order to get work, we would have to change our accents to sound like Americans.

After a couple of days in the hostel, and patiently calling English schools to be interviewed for English teaching jobs with no luck, I saw an advertisement 'Voiceover wanted'. It sounded interesting, although I had no idea what doing a voiceover involved. The money was very good. For four hours they would pay the equivalent of eighty Australian Dollars per hour. This was a small fortune as far as we were concerned. These were the days of no mobile phones, so I used the public telephone in the hostel to enquire about the job. The people recruiting for the voiceover position told me to meet them in the Hilton Hotel lobby. This seemed easy, as the Hilton Hotel was on the main road and was therefore easy to find. In the early days of arriving in Taipei I could not speak any Mandarin, so the easier a location was to find the better. My travelling companion waited for me at the hostel and I assured him I would come back later that day with some cash. We were both very excited.

I went off to the Hilton Hotel in my best clothes, which were drawstring pants and a cheap silk shirt which I had purchased in India, accessorised with pointy-toed leather sandals, which had also been purchased in India. The outfit looked good when I was travelling in India, but somehow did not translate when trying to impress for a job. I was met by two Chinese men at the Hilton Hotel. Two American men arrived for the meeting, who were obviously also being recruited for the voiceover position. I still had no idea what I had applied for.

The two Chinese men instructed us to follow them. The American men walked with confidence as though they had done this before and knew what the job entailed. I pretended to feel the same and did my best to also walk with confidence. When we were led down small Taiwanese alleys. I could not conceal my amazement because I had never seen anything like this. After about thirty minutes of walking through these fascinating streets – which unbeknown to me would be my home for the next five years – we arrived at a recording studio. Even though I had not started the job I was so excited about what I had already experienced. I could not wait to tell my travelling companion, although I still did not know what I was supposed to do. The men seated me in between the two American men behind large glass windows. Looking through these big glass windows gave me a sense of power, which proved to be short-lived.

We were handed scripts with the heading *Three's Company*. I had never heard of *Three's Company* and I had no idea it was a popular American sitcom. The Chinese guys on the other side of the glass windows operated the technology and instructed us to begin.

I said to the American guys, *"What am I supposed to do?"*

They replied in their thick American accents, *"Start your part of the script."* *"Where?"* I asked. They told me that I was Chrissy. I asked them, *"Who is Chrissy?"* They answered, *"She is the dumb blonde."* So I put on my best American accent and read the Chrissy script. Unfortunately, I could not act the dumb blonde. After a couple of hours of stopping and starting, because I did not know what I was doing, the Chinese men called me aside, paid me what was equivalent of AU$240, and told me to leave. The feeling of having so much money far outweighed my feelings of rejection.

After a week of staying in the hostel we found an apartment, sharing with four American students who had come to Taiwan to study Mandarin Chinese. They told us about their qualifications, but I had no idea what they were talking about. There was still an issue with finding an English teaching job because we had Australian accents.

So we learnt American phonetics, which guided us as to where to change our accents to sound authentic. After a few months of living in Taiwan we had gained a lot of experience in teaching English and were working in reputable English schools. I was teaching Chinese children English from 4pm - 6pm and then from 7pm - 9pm I would teach Chinese adult classes.

For the first year of living in Taiwan I spoke very little Mandarin. My main objective was to build my funds up. Eventually, I got tired of relying on Mandarin speakers for guidance. There was very little English spoken and most things were written in traditional Chinese characters. It got to the point where I could only communicate with people who spoke English, and not being able to read Chinese characters limited my world. So in my second year in Taiwan I joined Mandarin language classes in the morning from 10am - 12pm. Within six months my world changed. As well as speaking Mandarin, I could read many of the Chinese characters, which enabled me to get around the city much more easily.

My Chinese experience had now begun.

What does Guanxi mean

There is no English translation for *guanxi*. The closest meaning is 'relationships' or 'connections'. In Chinese culture, building your connections is a 24/7 activity, and therefore not restricted to your work environment. *Guanxi* can be developed anywhere, anytime. 'Relationship' in Chinese culture means a business relationship, and carries the same importance as a strong friendship, marriage or partnership. Building *guanxi* is a key ingredient in doing business with Chinese people, and it takes time and resources. Solid *guanxi* is viewed as long-term, and like any relationship, it takes effort to maintain. Chinese people often say 'no relationship, no business'. Most Chinese people start developing *guanxi* in their high school years; therefore, alumni networks play a very powerful role in Chinese society.

Guanxi does not involve the exchange of money; it is most often the exchange of a favour. *Guanxi* is a long-term commitment which may involve being asked to assist your Chinese contacts in situations that are not in your scope of knowledge or authority. Even if you know very little about the situation, it is important that you still make an attempt to help your Chinese contacts. You can do this by finding someone who has the expertise to help solve your Chinese contact's enquiry.

'Friends before business' is generally the business model for Chinese people. To achieve this business model, the lines between friends, business, work and leisure are often blurred. When dealing with Chinese people, developing *guanxi* is a good investment, and like any relationship, it takes some effort to create and to maintain.

Opportunistic Strategies

*I*n Book One of *The Dao of Negotiation – Tame the Tiger: Negotiating from a power position* we discussed the first six of the 36 Strategies, which are the **Advantageous Strategies**. In Book One I also spoke about the first part of my journey, and how I came to discover the 36 Strategies. These strategies are recognised as being at the core of Chinese thinking. Book One looks at some of the history of the strategies' origins, the meaning of the word *Dao*, the relevance of the words, and some basic facts that are crucial to functioning successfully in the Greater China Region.

Book Two – *Deceive the Dragon: Negotiating to retain power* discusses Strategies 7 – 12. These are the **Opportunistic Strategies.** These strategies can be played when you possess approximately the same strength or position as your opponent and must act to retain your power. The **Opportunistic Strategies** are best suited for situations where you will confront or be confronted. In these situations your opponent will be equally matched to you in terms of strength or power. These **Opportunistic Strategies** are deception strategies, and are used in situations where there are vulnerabilities that can be exploited. While many other strategies also use deception, this approach becomes more important in the **Opportunistic Strategies** because you do not have a strength advantage.

Most Western people do not get much practice at the game of negotiation, and learning these strategies with realistic examples will give readers an understanding of a structure that can be used to negotiate in any environment. To provide you with the best possible explanation of each strategy I provide the original story, which I then explain in contemporary English. You will then find examples of how each strategy can be played out on you and how to guard yourself against the strategy. I then show you how you can use the strategy. I have provided examples of how each strategy can be used in different environments.

Throughout *Deceive the Dragon: Negotiating to retain power* I refer to a fundamental Chinese cultural concept, which is *guanxi*. So you fully understand how this fits into Chinese culture and into the 36 Strategies, I have provided explanations of this important concept before introducing you to the **Opportunistic Strategies**.

Create something out of nothing means "to create an illusion out of something that does not exist"

You use the same feint twice. Having reacted to the first and often the second feint as well, your opponent will be hesitant to react to a third feint. Therefore, the third feint will be the actual attack, catching your enemy with his guard down.

During the Tang Dynasty in AD 755, General Zhang Xun had to defend his city, Yongqiu, against General Ling Huchao. General Zhang Xun was besieged, and his army was quickly running out of food, water and arrows for ammunition. In fact, it looked as though he was going to be defeated, and Yongqui would be taken over by General Ling Huchao. To survive, General Zhang Xun commanded his troops to make one thousand straw dummies and dress them in black. The dummies had little chance of being detected in the dark of the night, so at midnight he ordered them to be tied to ropes and lowered over the walls of Yongqui.

General Ling Huchao's troops thought the dummies were real people coming over the wall from inside the city, and instinctively attacked by shooting thousands of arrows into their bodies. General Zhang Xun then ordered the dummies to be pulled back to the inside of the city, where the thousands of arrows from the dummies were collected to replenish the ammunition supplies. Shortly after this incident General Zhang Xun ordered 500 of his men to climb over the city walls to defend the city against General Ling Huchao's army, and this time real people were attacking.

General Ling Huchao's troops assumed these real people were also dummies, and as they were not going to be tricked again, they turned away from this attack and laughed, thinking they had outwitted General Zhang Xun's troops. Zhang Xun's 500 men conquered the opposing side using the arrows that they had collected from the first attack, which was a feint. By using Strategy Seven - **Create Something out of nothing**, General Zhang Xun was able to defend his city so it was not taken over by General Ling Huchao.

In this situation General Zhang Xun defended his city, Yongqiu, against General Ling Huchao by using a '*feint*'. Sometimes when Strategy Seven is used the strategist '*uses the same feint twice*'. However, in this case the feint was only used once. When General Ling Huchao knew the '*first feint*' was made up of dummies he thought the next attack was also a feint, and he therefore was '*hesitant to react*', however this was '*the actual attack*'.

When Strategy Seven is used, the strategist creates an illusion when there is, in fact, nothing there. Once this illusion is performed one or two times, you discover it is not real. When Strategy Seven is used on you for the final time the situation is likely to be ignored, because you may think it will not be real, just like the previous times. However, the final time is real, and because you think it is fake you '*drop your guard*', which leaves you unprepared for the '*actual situation*'.

Negotiating with Chinese People

EXAMPLE ONE
Strategy Seven in action (against you)

When visiting China and meeting with Chinese business people, part of the *guanxi* development is to invite your Chinese contacts to visit you in your country. Strategy Seven may be played out on you when you return to your country, and your contacts agree to take up your kind offer to visit you. When using Strategy Seven your Chinese contacts might tell you they are arriving, with no real intention of visiting, which '*creates a feint*'. Your natural instinct is to believe them and prepare everything for their arrival, which includes meeting arrangements and allocating time out of your schedule to look after your Chinese guests.

Then two weeks before their arrival, they cancel their trip and give you the excuse that all travelling decisions are out of their control. A short time after cancelling, your Chinese contacts make contact with you again to inform you that they are again planning to visit, which is now the '*second feint*' because once again they cancel, and just like the first time you have prepared arrangements for their arrival. After preparing everything for the second time, you decide the next time this happens, there will be no preparation and no more time wasted on this group.

By taking this attitude, problems could arise when your Chinese contacts inform you for the third time that they are coming to visit. You might be *'hesitant to react'* because past experience says they will not arrive, so you are likely to prepare very little for their arrival. However, when applying Strategy Seven, this is the *'actual visit'*, and by thinking this was the same as the first two proposed visits, you prepare very little for their arrival. During the communication you have had with your Chinese contacts in the planning of the first two proposed visits, it is likely they will have learned information about you and are therefore aware of your strengths and weaknesses. When they arrive, you find yourself in a disorganised situation, and it is likely that your Chinese guests will have the upper hand in meetings and other business discussions, because you are consumed with trying to organise their trip at the last minute. Your energy is then depleted by trying to do your best to make an unanticipated situation go smoothly.

EXAMPLE ONE
Guarding yourself against Strategy Seven

When your Chinese contacts inform you that they are planning to visit always be prepared. Even though they inform you they are visiting, it is likely they will cancel *'the first and often the second time'* before the actual visit. Make sure you are prepared every time.

EXAMPLE TWO
Strategy Seven in action (against you)

Many wine companies want to export their wine to China, and locating a reputable distributor is one of the critical keys in setting up an export business. A scenario may be that a wine company has connected with a reputable distributor in Shanghai, and this distributor seems like a good choice, as they have links into other provinces in China and also have a good reputation for supporting their foreign suppliers. The distributor wants the wine company to visit their office in China to meet them personally before discussing a possible deal. So the wine company sends their Business Development Manager and Marketing Manager to China to meet with the distributor's General Manager.

The Business Development Manager and the Marketing Manager are fully prepared for the meeting, and arrive at the Shanghai office excited about these export possibilities. When applying Strategy Seven, the staff at the distributor's office talk with the people from the wine company, give them tea, and are generally very friendly, which is the preparation for the '*first feint*'. Often in this situation the foreign company is keen to develop *guanxi*, so they talk about their company and the conversation moves into areas such as prices. Then, after a long wait for the General Manager to arrive, they are informed that the General Manager is returning from America and the plane has been delayed.

The distribution office asks the wine company to return the next day at the same time. The General Manager should be back, and the flights will hopefully be back to normal. Notice when applying Strategy Seven they use the words 'should' and 'hopefully', which leaves the manager open for another no-show, and therefore to apply the *second feint*. As instructed, the Business Development Manager and the Marketing Manager arrive at the distributor's office at the agreed time. Once again, the same thing happens. They sit in the office and drink tea and talk with the staff about their wine. The staff make a few phone calls and then inform the wine company, after another lengthy wait, that the General Manager is still at the airport but will definitely be in the office the next day to meet with them.

The Business Development Manager and the Marketing Manager now feel that their time has been wasted, and without realising it, they have given away a lot of information during informal conversations with the Chinese staff during the visits to their office on the previous days. In this situation, Strategy Three - **Murder with a borrowed knife,** from Book One – *Tame the Tiger: Negotiating from a power position* is used, where staff at a lower level are used to deliver unexpected news. The use of Strategy Three assists the successful application of Strategy Seven. As they are very disappointed and think that the General Manager will probably not turn up for the meeting the next morning, the foreign wine company decide that only the Business Development Manager will go to the meeting and the Marketing Manager will stay at the hotel and do some work, as they feel they have already wasted a lot of time.

The Business Development Manager goes to the meeting, not expecting the General Manager to be there. To their surprise the General Manager is at the office fully prepared for the meeting as this is the *'actual meeting'*. The wine company representative then feels embarrassed because they had told the General Manager there would be two people at the meeting, but the Marketing Manager is not present. The distribution company now has a lot of information about the wine company through the discussions they had with the staff during the previous visits, which were the *'first and second feint'*. The third visit is the *'actual meeting'*, and because they have extracted information out of the wine company, the distributor has the upper hand with regards to issues such as price and delivery.

EXAMPLE TWO
Guarding yourself against Strategy Seven

In this scenario you may feel as though the meeting will never be organised and you are tired of returning to the office, because the person you want to see does not turn up. When working with Chinese people, patience is important, as it is likely that one or several of the 36 Strategies will be played out on you. During the *'first and second feint'* do not give away too much information. Keep the conversation friendly and discuss everything except the business, and in this way you do not run the risk of giving away valuable information. When the third meeting is organised, treat this meeting just as seriously as any *'actual meeting'*.

Key Points when Strategy Seven is used against you

- Be careful what you say in every meeting.
- Treat every proposed meeting as the actual meeting.
- Do not give away too much information during the lead up to the actual meeting.

Example Three
Enacting Strategy Seven

You can use Strategy Seven on your Chinese contacts by inviting them to Australia and when they arrive for the first meeting do not discuss business. However, you can mention in your correspondence to them that you are looking forward to discussing business. You create an expectation, so they will probably expect you to talk about business issues during the first meeting. To apply Strategy Seven in this first meeting, you serve food and drinks to your visitors and display yourself as the perfect host, discussing everything except business. You are applying Strategy Seven by using a *'feint'* in the first meeting, and the *'feint'* is that you told your Chinese guests that you will be discussing business. However, you did not tell them precisely when this would happen. You can use this first meeting to observe their personalities, including their strengths and weaknesses, so you will know how to deal with them in the *'actual meeting'*, where you will discuss business issues.

On the second meeting with your Chinese contacts, which will probably be the next day, to apply Strategy Seven and therefore the '*second feint*', you take them out to dinner and once again do not discuss business. After eating and drinking you escort them back to their hotel and inform them you will pick them up the next morning for a meeting. By this time you have learnt a lot about your Chinese contacts, and now know more about dealing with them in preparation for the '*feint*'.

Then, the third meeting, which is the '*actual meeting*' takes place, and because things have not been serious in the previous meetings your Chinese group may not be prepared for a meeting where you talk about business. By applying Strategy Seven you can gain information about the personalities of the group and also create a situation where they will not be aware when the '*actual meeting*' will take place.

Negotiating in a Western Environment

EXAMPLE FOUR
Enacting Strategy Seven

A situation may be that you are a franchisor and you are selling individual franchises. A way of introducing potential customers to purchase your franchises is through an information evening. When the guests arrive at your information evening they are often expecting to have a presentation about income and the rules and regulations of buying a franchise. To apply Strategy Seven in the information evening, you '*create a feint*' by talking about the empowering feeling of being your own boss. Therefore, you do not talk about cashflow and other financial concerns that may drive them away from planning to purchase a franchise. The strategy behind discussing only lifestyle in the first instance is to get the potential buyer's confidence. Then, after getting to know them, discuss the issues about the costs involved when purchasing a franchise, which will be the '*actual meeting*'. Your potential buyers will not expect this, and they are likely to have '*their guard down*'. During the time spent discussing topics such as lifestyle you get to know the personalities of your audience and have a better idea of how to approach the subject of money.

Key Points when using Strategy Seven

- When first meeting potential buyers it is better to keep clear of talking about money.
- Use the first meeting to learn about the personalities of your potential customers.
- After you have gotten to know your potential customers' personalities, then discuss the more challenging conversations such as money.

Openly repair the walkway, secretly march to Chencang means *"pretend to advance down one path while taking another hidden path"*

Attack the enemy with two convergent forces. The first is the direct attack, one that is obvious and for which the enemy prepares his defences. The second is the indirect sinister attack that the enemy does not expect and which causes him to divide his forces at the last minute, leading to confusion and disaster.

*A*t the end of the Qin Dynasty, in 208 BC, there was a battle between Liu Bang and Xiang Yu. During this battle Liu Bang was forced to retreat to Sichuan Province. Liu Bang destroyed the road and all its bridges to Sichuan so that Xiang Yu could not follow his army. When he felt ready to march out of Sichuan and resume the war, Liu Bang applied Strategy Eight - **Openly repair the walkway, secretly marching to Chencang** and began to openly repair the road he had destroyed. Xiang Yu decided Liu Bang was not likely to move out of Sichuan Province until he had completed the repairs to this road, and so did not attack him at this time. Xiang Yu and his army hid and watched the bridges being gradually restored, and prepared his army for Liu Bang's retaliation. Even when most of the bridges were restored, Xiang Yu could see no sign of Liu Bang's army moving forward. However, knowing that Xiang Yu was watching him, Liu Bang used the little known Chencang passage out of Sichuan and took Xiang Yu by surprise, which led to the defeat of Xiang Yu by Liu Bang.

In this situation, the first move was for Liu Bang to rebuild the road out of Sichuan in the open, which was '*obvious*', and this move drove Xiang Yu to prepare his defences. He prepared his army for when Liu Bang would use this road. However, Liu Bang did not use this obvious road, but rather an alternative unexpected route, and this was an '*indirect attack*', which caused Xiang Yu to divide his forces at the last minute, '*leading to confusion and disaster*'.

When Strategy Eight is used on you, the strategist creates a situation where the person they are dealing with is led to think that the strategist will take an obvious path. They then surprise the person when they apply Strategy Eight, by taking another, unanticipated path, which causes confusion.

Strategy Eight may appear to be the same as Strategy Six – **Make a noise in the east and attack in the west,** from Book One - *Tame the Tiger: Negotiating from a power position.* However, Strategy Eight is an extension of Strategy Six, because while Strategy Six provides you with misinformation to draw your attention away from the main issue, Strategy Eight not only gives you misinformation, it also uses physical evidence to make this incorrect information seem more convincing. Strategy Eight is focused on hiding the actual route of the strategy by openly revealing a deceptive route, in order to protect the real path of the strategy, whereas Strategy Six is focused on hiding the immediate issue.

Negotiating with Chinese People

EXAMPLE ONE
Strategy Eight in action (against you)

Often when Western companies travel to China to source products it is overwhelming to see how large these Chinese companies are, compared to companies in their own country. What is described as a reasonably large company in the West can be perceived as relatively small in China. A Western company may be sourcing items of machinery from China for their business. The reason they are trying to buy these items from China is that from extensive research they know they can buy what they need for a much cheaper price. The advice people often take with them before they search China for what they want is to look for Chinese companies that are already operating internationally. Chinese companies already trading globally will be knowledgeable regarding shipping, quality assurance, intellectual property laws, and other issues. They are also likely to have people who have a reasonable command of English because of their dealings with English speaking countries. All of this information is essential to be aware of when sourcing products from China.

During this process it is likely that the Western company will visit several factories and have an array of questions they need to ask. Once the Chinese company answers these questions they are then considered a likely candidate to purchase from. If you are a Western company and a Chinese company is interested in selling you the goods, you may be of interest to them because you are their road into your country of origin. They want to '*openly repair the walkway and secretly march to your country*', and therefore they may have limited interest in taking you on as their customer, because their main interest is in getting contacts in your country. So be aware that they may have another agenda. In this scenario, the Western company is sent the goods they have ordered and everything goes smoothly for a while. Then, after a short time, the company receiving the goods may notice that the Chinese company is not providing the same customer services as they did in the past. The Chinese company is applying Strategy Eight where they wanted an inroad into the Western country. If you are not aware of Strategy Eight, this scenario can leave you '*confused*' as to why this has happened.

EXAMPLE ONE
Guarding yourself against Strategy Eight

When you go to China to source products, keep in mind that the Chinese company you are dealing with may be '*openly repairing a walkway and secretly marching to your country*'. This means they may not be particularly interested in selling you the goods you want, but rather they may be using you to get to where they want to go. Essentially there is nothing wrong with this, as you are still likely to get what you want. However, the importance of dealing with you may diminish, and because they have less interest in dealing with your company you may feel let down and therefore '*confused*'.

It is a good idea to have more than one supplier, because if Strategy Eight is played out on you it may become difficult to communicate with the single supplier, as their focus will be more on connecting with other potential customers and establishing some substantial business in your country, with the possibility of getting much larger buyers of their products. So it is wise to have two or three suppliers to guard against this strategy. Also, if you are aware Strategy Eight is being played out on you, this knowledge will guard you against any potential '*confusion*'.

EXAMPLE TWO
Strategy Eight in action (against you)

In China, many Western companies are often perceived as being very innovative. This is particularly the case in the services and training areas. You may be a Western company visiting China with a management training program which China is very interested in. This is likely to be very unique in China, and the companies you visit are very interested in what you have available. The course may include popular topics, such as project management and emotional intelligence, which are of interest to the contemporary Chinese workplace.

The situation may be that you have seen several companies and have chosen one company whom you feel comfortable dealing with. The meetings are quite long, and you have participated in a lot of dinners and have established solid *guanxi*. However, there has been no money exchanged, and little talk of money. You are aware that your training programs are quite expensive, but you also know these courses are unique in China, and you are confident that cost will not be a huge issue.

During these discussions you share several of your training outlines and go through the content, and you also think that you have been very thorough by getting them to sign confidentiality agreements. By this stage they know a lot about your courses, the methodology that underpins them, duration of delivery and other issues that add to the successful delivery of your courses.

After sharing this information you go back to your own country on the understanding that everything will begin to go ahead very soon. After further discussions via email you receive an email from the assistant manager, which states that at this stage they will not be going ahead with purchasing your courses, due to structural reasons within the company. They are very polite and thank you for your time. They use Strategy Three - **Murder with a borrowed Knife** from Book One – *Tame the Tiger: Negotiating from a position of power*, because it is the assistant manager who will deliver the news, and not the manager whom you have dealt with.

The company now know a lot about your training courses, and are clear they are not breaching the boundaries of the confidentiality agreement. If they have the right skills they now have enough knowledge to run these courses themselves. During all of your negotiations you were not aware of anyone in this company with the skills to organise and deliver your courses, so you conclude that it is all fine. What you did not know is that the Chinese company had someone in their company who had been educated in a Western country in the area of training and development. During the process of communication they have learnt many things about your courses. In the meantime, while this was happening, you put your time and energy into thinking they would be using your courses and there was no consideration that there may be a possibility that they were using Strategy Eight. You did not 'expect this' which left you in a 'confused state'.

EXAMPLE TWO
Guarding yourself against Strategy Eight

If you are selling a product or service to a Chinese company and you are aware that what you have is very unique, be careful not to let your confidence and passion about the product you are selling override the possibility of Strategy Eight being played out on you. Even though it looks like you have completed discussions and you feel your company is the one they want to deal with, do not be too complacent about thinking that you are the only one who can deliver these courses. Think of all of the reasons as to why the Chinese company want to show they are interested in what you have, because one of the reasons may be to learn about your offerings and then deliver it themselves. Know the boundaries about what you are telling your Chinese contacts. You need to tell them enough so they are interested, but not too much so that they take the information and do it themselves. Remember, Chinese people live in an environment where negotiation is happening in their daily life, so they are experts at working out how to get the best deal. Like any smart business person, if they can do it themselves, they will.

Key Points when Strategy Eight is used against you

- Be aware there may be other objectives for Chinese people to build *guanxi* with you, apart from just wanting to do business with your company.
- Have two or three suppliers or contacts that you are dealing with to guard yourself against just being the road to something else.
- Be careful not to give away important details before a deal is done.

EXAMPLE THREE
Enacting Strategy Eight

A scenario may be that you have invited your Chinese contacts to visit, and you have a suspicion they are seeing other businesses, who are your competitors, while they are visiting your country. In this situation you also feel that you have not impressed them enough in order for them to be interested in what you are selling, and therefore feel vulnerable and think they may prefer your competitors. We can use the example of wine as there are lots of companies exporting wine to China, making it a highly competitive industry. To apply Strategy Eight where you '*openly repair the walkway*', you pick your Chinese contacts up at the airport. After this initial meeting they think you are taking them to their hotel, however, you have secretly arranged to take them to one of your reliable business contact's offices. En route back to their hotel you take them to visit your colleague, who has been instructed to praise your wine and talk about the great reputation it has on the international market. You are also aware it is very important in Chinese culture for your colleague to discuss the reputation of your wine in front of your Chinese guests, as they will feel they are meeting a well-known company. In this scenario, Strategy Eight has been used to create an impression by 'secretly going to a place', where your friend's office is, and they will assist with your marketing by creating a positive impression. Your Chinese guests will not expect this, and may be '*confused*' about this diversion. However, this visit to your colleague's office may provide another step towards the decision to encourage them to purchase your wine. After Strategy Eight has been enacted you take them back to their hotel and do not mention the visit to your colleague's offices. They may mention something about this visit over dinner that night. Just listen, allow them to talk and let Strategy Eight do its work.

Negotiating in a Western Environment

EXAMPLE FOUR
Enacting Strategy Eight

A useful situation where Strategy Eight can be employed is when accepting a job offer that is not exactly the job the candidate wants. One scenario may be that a recently qualified accountant has dreams of working for one of the top-tier accounting firms, but does not have enough experience to secure a position with them. Instead, this accountant applies for a job in a middle-level accounting firm and gets the job. In the interview this accountant explains all the reasons why they want to work at this mid-level firm, and states that they are incredibly excited by this opportunity. While the accountant is being interviewed for the job, this mid-level accounting company can only see they will employ a new graduate who will be an asset for the company, and do not envisage that Strategy Eight is being enacted. Therefore, this accounting firm can only see the direct path of the accountant; that is, to work for them. While the accountant has every intention of working for them, they are also constructing plans to take another path in order to work for a much larger firm. They are enacting Strategy Eight by *'openly taking this position and then secretly marching to another company'*. The accountant gains valuable skills, works hard to make sure they will have a great reference, and networks with influential people. While they are working within the smaller firm they are making contacts with larger accounting firms, until they are able to apply for a position with one of the top-tier companies that they have always wanted to work for. If the smaller firm does not see Strategy Eight is being used on them, they will be unprepared for when the accountant leaves their company and left 'confused'.

Key Points when using Strategy Eight

- Hide your real intentions behind harmless actions.
- Create good impressions by taking your contacts to a colleague's office, where your colleague will speak highly of you.
- Use your direct path to make yourself look better, and gain skills or information, in order to take your indirect path.

Watching the fire on the opposite shore
means *"patiently watching a situation unfold then making your move"*

Delay entering the field of battle until all the other players have become exhausted by fighting amongst themselves. Then go in full strength and pick up the pieces.

*D*uring the period of the Three Kingdoms, in a battle, Cao Cao defeated Yuan Shao. Yuan Shao had three sons and after Yuan Shao's defeat, his sons began to argue amongst themselves as to who would be his successor. The eldest son was angry because Yuan Shao chose his middle son as his successor, a decision that caused conflict between the sons. In order to eliminate his enemy completely, Cao Cao decided that he would attack the three brothers. However, when he began to mobilise his troops to attack, the brothers came together as a group to protect themselves. Cao Cao then applied Strategy Nine - **Watching the fire on the opposite shore**, by withdrawing his plans of attack and therefore '*delaying entering the field of battle*', because he presumed that if he waited, Yuan Shao's three sons would go back to '*fighting amongst themselves*', and this would weaken their defence. Cao Cao's prediction was correct. The infighting between the brothers escalated to the point where the two younger brothers beheaded the eldest brother.

As the conflict between the brothers continued, Cao Cao began to attack the outer regions of the brothers' territory, as he was able to '*go in with full strength and pick up the pieces*' without competition. The Yuan brothers became aware of Cao Cao's strength and feared an attack, so they fled to Liaodong. Cao Cao's general advised him to kill the Yuan brothers and then conquer Liaodong. Cao Cao again decided to '*delay entering the field of battle*', because he was aware that the Lord of Liaodong disliked the Yuan brothers. The Yuan brothers sought the Lord of Liaodong's assistance to fight against Cao Cao. The Lord of Liaodong was doubtful of such an alliance, because he knew that if Cao Cao attacked he would have to join forces with the Yuan brothers, whom he did not like. However, he also knew that if Cao Cao did not attack, the brothers would eventually take over Liaodong. When he realised that Cao Cao was not going to attack he had the Yuan brothers beheaded and sent their heads to Cao Cao as a peace offering.

When Strategy Nine is applied, the strategist exploits the internal divisions of an otherwise united group. They do this by refraining from intervening until the disputes have exhausted the group, and then the strategist can '*go in full strength and pick up the pieces*'.

Strategy Nine may look like Strategy Five – **Loot a burning house,** from Book One - *Tame the Tiger:*

Negotiating from a position of power. However, the difference is that Strategy Five involves a crisis where the strategist looks for opportunities in that crisis. Strategy Nine is about patiently watching an internal dispute play out within a group. The strategist moves in to get what they want once the group has exhausted themselves from their internal conflict.

Negotiating with Chinese People

EXAMPLE ONE
Strategy Nine in action (against you)

When Strategy Nine is used on you, your company is likely to be in a situation where there have been several meetings involving negotiations with your Chinese counterparts, and during these negotiations your team has experienced some internal conflict or disagreement. This internal disagreement will have nothing to do with the negotiation with the Chinese company. Rather, it may be about your political differences, your salary or the working conditions within your company. To apply Strategy Nine, your Chinese counterparts will not comment, even if you ask them for their opinion. They will *'watch you become exhausted while you fight amongst yourselves'*. Then, after you have exhausted yourselves, they will *'go in full strength and pick up the pieces'*.

The reality is that if you are in a negotiation and have exhausted yourselves through these internal conflicts, you are likely to lack the mental energy to think through what the best outcome is for your company. This situation may split up your team as a result of the dispute. As your Chinese counterparts observe you they may have been waiting for this situation to happen, so they can deal with a weaker team by *'going in full strength and picking up the pieces'*.

EXAMPLE ONE
Guarding yourself against Strategy Nine

If you have an internal dispute within your company when you are dealing with your Chinese contacts, it is important not to discuss this dispute with your Chinese contacts, even if you become very friendly with them. Discussing any internal dispute with your Chinese contacts will give them the opportunity to apply Strategy Nine. Resolve your internal disputes prior to meeting your Chinese counterparts, and even if you have not resolved your disputes, do not discuss these issues with your Chinese contacts, and never ask their opinion about the situation. Western people often feel that discussing these topics would be a way of developing *guanxi* with their Chinese contacts. It is important to continue to develop *guanxi*, however, you need to be careful what topics you are using for the relationship development. Even if it feels right, avoid discussing any internal conflicts or disputes, and you will guard yourself against having Strategy Nine used on you.

EXAMPLE TWO
Strategy Nine in action (against you)

For Strategy Nine to be used on you by your Chinese counterparts, be aware that they will have taken the time to conduct extensive research on your company. This research often gives them a good understanding of the conflicts that exist within your internal environment. There are many industries from Western countries that are aiming to get into the China market. These industry sectors include aged care, retirement, wine, agribusiness, childcare, education and many other industry sectors. All of these industry sectors have competitors within their industry that are striving to enter China. Often these competitors have disputes as to who is offering the best product. It is common for businesses to believe their product is the best, because it is this passion and belief in the product that drives innovation and entrepreneurship. Often it is this passionate energy that encourages a business within an industry to talk about their business to their Chinese contacts as being of a higher quality compared to their competitors.

Many Western universities want to market their courses to China. Competition between universities is fierce, and this competition often leads to the situation where universities are in conflict over the courses they offer. Such a situation gives Chinese education agents the opportunity to apply Strategy Nine, which is a wait and see attitude, while the Western universities are in conflict with each other. The Chinese education agent can then '*pick up the pieces after the universities have become exhausted*' from these conflicts. The result is that the Chinese education agent gets the course offered for a good price. When applying Strategy Nine, Chinese education agents will wait for the best deals for foreign courses.

EXAMPLE TWO
Guarding yourself against Strategy Nine

You may feel passionate about your product and want to describe it as the best in the market. However, when discussing your product with Chinese people it is beneficial to also speak highly of your competitors. This style of communication will not give your Chinese contacts the opportunity to apply Strategy Nine. There are often disagreements and disputes between businesses inside industry sectors. If you have conflicts with other businesses inside your industry sector do not disclose or discuss this with your Chinese contacts. In Western culture people often discuss disagreements openly, whereas in Chinese business culture this is not only a culturally inappropriate way of communicating, it is also a way of giving your Chinese contacts the space to apply Strategy Nine against you.

> **Key Points when Strategy Nine is used against you**
> - If your team is having an internal dispute do not discuss this with your Chinese contacts.
> - If you are having disagreements with competitors in your industry sector do not discuss this with your Chinese contacts, rather, give your competitors a compliment.
> - Be aware that your Chinese contacts will cleverly watch you use up your energy from your internal company dispute or industry disputes.

EXAMPLE THREE
Enacting Strategy Nine

When you are planning to export your product to China, if you want to apply Strategy Nine, you will need to conduct extensive research on your Chinese contacts. A scenario may be that you are planning to export a food product such as milk formula. This product was in high demand in China during the 2008 milk formula contamination issue. The consumption of this contaminated product left many children in China with permanent organ damage. Demand for products fluctuates depending on what is going on in the market, which is why it is important to conduct research.

If you are entering the Chinese market for the first time, one effective method using Strategy Nine is to attend an exhibition or trade show. This will give you the opportunity to see products on display that are similar to yours, and to meet distributors and see what your competitors are marketing in

China. If you are planning to export food products you can collect samples, take photos, and collect brochures and any other marketing materials your competitors are displaying.

The next step is to visit Chinese stores that are selling a similar product to yours. By doing this you will be able to see what Chinese people are buying and which products are most popular with Chinese consumers. This is applying Strategy Nine because you are '*delaying entering the Chinese market*' until you have carried out as much research as you can. You may discover that you need to modify your product to make it more attractive to the Chinese consumer. Once you have researched this information you can then search for a suitable distributor, as you will have a clearer idea about where your product is likely to sell and also other issues, such as appropriate pricing and packaging.

As there are many distributors in China this area is very competitive, and there are often disputes between distributors. If the distributor attempts to draw you into a conversation regarding a dispute they are having with their competitors, do not enter this conversation. Apply Strategy Nine by watching the distributors '*exhaust themselves through fighting amongst themselves*'.

By researching the market and attending exhibitions and trade shows, observing what is being sold in the Chinese stores, understanding what your potential Chinese consumer is interested in, and looking for the right distributor without entering any of their competitor conflicts, you are applying Strategy Nine. The application of Strategy Nine provides you with a much better chance of making the right choice for a long-term successful plan. When you are observing what is going on you will have the space to be aware of conflicts between distributors, and this also allows you time to adjust your product to meet the cultural and linguistic needs of the Chinese market.

Negotiating in a Western Environment

EXAMPLE FOUR
Enacting Strategy Nine

You can enact Strategy Nine by watching a new product as it arrives onto the market before you purchase it. An example may be when a new iPhone is released. There is always a rush to be the first in line to purchase it. If you enact Strategy Nine you will *'delay buying this new model'* until all of the problems have been identified and resolved. You are watching from a distance. In most cases when a new piece of technology is released there are problems, and so by applying Strategy Nine you will see if these problems have been resolved before you purchase. You can then decide if you really want to purchase this new product. As you have waited to see how well the product is doing, you may decide not to purchase this particular phone. By enacting Strategy Nine you will have the chance to make better choices about purchasing new products entering the market, and therefore not buy the problems that other consumers have encountered.

Key Points when using Strategy Nine

- Do your own research before making any decisions.
- Adopt a 'wait and see' attitude.
- Delay purchasing a product until you research the consumer feedback.

Strategy Ten

Hide your dagger behind a smile means *"to hide your real intentions"*

Charm and ingratiate yourself with your enemy. When you have gained his trust, you move against him in secret.

To conquer the state of Hu, the ruler of Wu used Strategy Ten – **Hide your dagger behind a smile**. He did this by first arranging for his daughter to marry the prince of Hu, which brought him closer to and better able to build *guanxi* with the rulers of Hu. After his daughter married the Prince of Hu, the ruler of Wu was perceived as a trustworthy person. The ruler of Wu '*charmed and ingratiated himself*' with the Prince of Hu.

His aim was to conquer the state of Hu, and one of his advisers suggested directly attacking the Territory of Hu. The ruler of Wu used his adviser's suggestion as another means of applying Strategy Ten. Even though he wanted to attack the state of Hu, he outwardly expressed fury at his adviser's suggestion, and then publically beheaded his adviser for giving him this advice. He correctly predicted this news would be well received in Hu. He once again '*charmed and ingratiated himself*' with the Prince of Hu. When the Prince of Hu heard this news he was very grateful, as he perceived that there was strong and trusting *guanxi* between the rulers of Hu and the rulers of Wu, with Wu now an ally of Hu.

After marrying the ruler of Wu's daughter and hearing about the beheading of the ruler of Wu's adviser, the Prince of Hu had full trust in the ruler of Wu. Once the ruler of Wu had '*gained his trust, he moved against him in secret*'. It was then that the ruler of Wu attacked and conquered the state of Hu.

When Strategy Ten is used, its purpose is to relax the person the strategy is applied on, and when they are relaxed and therefore see the strategist as no threat, the strategist then surprises them with a situation they are not ready for. This results in the strategist having the upper hand.

The communication method in Chinese culture is mostly indirect. If someone is not interested in what you are offering they are not likely to tell you 'no' directly. Applying Strategy Ten is often used to ensure the *guanxi* continues to grow. This means that a Chinese business person may say 'yes' to an offer when they actually mean 'no', and then the person marketing to the Chinese person is disappointed when the Chinese person does not get back to them. The reason for the 'yes' answer is to continue to develop the *guanxi*, even though there may be no interest in what the person is offering. *Guanxi* is one of the most important components of Chinese business culture and is often put ahead of everything else related to the deal.

Strategy Ten may look similar to Strategy Eight – **Openly repair the walkway, secretly march to Chencang**. However, Strategy Ten is about not saying what you may really mean in order to keep the connection, whereas Strategy Eight is about taking someone down one path, so they do not see the real path the strategist is actually using.

The application of Strategy Ten is also used in difficult circumstances where the strategist uses empathy in situations such as those where people are made redundant. Strategy Ten is applied by telling them only the positive things about their work, so the reputations and dignity of these people made redundant are preserved.

Negotiating with Chinese People

EXAMPLE ONE
Strategy Ten in action (against you)

One way for Western products to enter the China market is for a Western company to join a delegation that departs from their country and travels to China as a group. This is often a good way of entering China, especially if the company is new to China. In this scenario, business meetings are arranged by the organisers of the delegation. Many newcomers to China are not aware that when they present their product to a Chinese company, the Chinese company may say 'yes' they are interested, when they actually mean 'no'. By saying 'yes' the Chinese company is applying Strategy Ten. When receiving this reaction the Western company often feels they have really impressed the Chinese company, and feel confident the Chinese company is interested in what they have to offer. The Western company presumes it is just a matter of returning to their country and organising an order to be sent to China, and they feel they have successfully entered the Chinese market. The Western company then thinks, 'How easy was that?', but in reality their judgement is incorrect. They have been '*charmed and ingratiated*' by these potential Chinese customers.

Strategy Ten is used on many industry sectors including wine, childcare, aged care, environmental technology, agribusiness and many more. Even if the sector you are operating in is sought after, do not just assume that because there is demand for your product or service your Chinese contacts will be interested in what you have to offer. Quite often in the situation where they are not interested they are still likely to say 'yes' when they actually mean 'no' so that they can build *guanxi*.

EXAMPLE ONE
Guarding yourself against Strategy Ten

When you present your product to a potential Chinese buyer you are more than likely to be one of the many Western companies who have presented to these companies. *Guanxi*, which is a key component of Chinese communication, overrides telling you directly that they are not interested in your products. They would often prefer to tell you 'yes' even if it is just to keep the relationship alive. Chinese people have a saying 'One more road offers one more connection'. In Chinese culture the more connections you have the more effective you will be in the business world.

It will be more beneficial if you do not question the Chinese people's indirect style of communication. In Western culture a 'yes' means 'yes' and a 'no' means 'no'. Once you know that Strategy Ten is being played out on you, do not judge your contacts on their indirect answer when they say 'yes' and they really mean 'no'. Understand that this is a different way of communicating, and there is a strategy in action. Do not question or try to challenge their answer. Understand this is a method of building *guanxi*.

One way to detect if the 'yes' means 'yes' or 'no' is to observe if your contact is saying 'yes' without any enquiry about your product. This probably means that they are not really interested. If they are asking many questions about what you are selling this may mean they are interested and the 'yes' may really mean 'yes'. As this is a very common strategy in Chinese business, it is wise to firstly presume your contact is not interested. By thinking in this way you are not setting yourself up for disappointment. Understand that most of the time it takes a lot more than one meeting to make a sale in China. It is important not to judge the communication style primarily on your own Western way of communicating, rather, understand you are dealing with a different culture, and even though these different ways of answering may seem inappropriate, there is a reason as to why Chinese people answer in this way. Remember that Strategy Ten is often being played out *'when they have gained your trust'*, making you vulnerable.

EXAMPLE TWO
Strategy Ten in action (against you)

Strategy Ten can be used on you when you have been *'charmed'* and *'your trust has been gained'*. A likely scenario for when Strategy Ten will be used is when you visit China for the first time on a trade mission with several other delegates from your country. You plan to market your meat products to a reputable distributor in China. After meeting with twenty Chinese distributors who have the capacity to market your meat products in China, in your opinion you have made some excellent contacts. However, you are aware that Strategy Ten is in action, and with this knowledge you know that even though eighteen of these Chinese companies have indicated they are strongly interested, because they have said a convincing 'yes', you are aware that they are likely to really mean 'no'. Through analysing how these distributors communicated with you, you have narrowed the choice of contacts to three. In this scenario you can clearly see Strategy Ten has been played out on you. However, you do not realise Strategy Ten will be played out on you again in your follow up visit to China.

Your next step is to visit China to meet with these three chosen distributors. These three Chinese distributors are located in different cities in China, which are Shanghai, Beijing and Qingdao. This time you visit China with your business partner and do not have the advice and support of the government delegation, as you did on your previous trip. Your first stop is to visit the distributor in Shanghai.

This distributor picks you up at the airport, buys you lovely dinners and gives you beautiful gifts. These actions ensure you feel very comfortable, so you are in a relaxed state of mind. In this situation, Strategy Ten is being applied and you are being '*charmed by the Chinese distributor*'. There is no discussion about the price of your product being too high, and you are delighted with the hospitality and assume that everything is fine regarding the price. This puts you in a state where you are relaxed and feel you can trust this distributor. As this has been a very positive meeting you are not too concerned about how the next two meetings in Beijing and Qingdao will work out. You know that building *guanxi* is crucial when developing contacts in China, so therefore you feel you are beginning to understand China and have made great progress in this very first meeting. In the hope of developing the relationship even more, you change your ticket so you can revisit Shanghai after you have been to Beijing and Qingdao.

You visit the other two distributors in Beijing and Qingdao, and you are not impressed because you do not experience the same level of hospitality as you did with the company in Shanghai. Not only this, but these companies query your prices and are ask numerous questions regarding logistics, which is causing you to feel confronted and uncomfortable.

When you return to visit the chosen Shanghai distributor, just before you arrive, the company informs you that you will need to get yourself to the hotel and they will meet you there. This is in stark contrast to the previous visit's hospitality. However, you are not concerned, as your judgement has been clouded by the previous visit. At the hotel you wait for your contact in the foyer, and two people from the Chinese distribution company arrive to meet you. These people are not the people you met on the previous visit; in fact, you have not heard of or met these people before. These people are not senior level people, and you have been told that something important arose and the people you met with last time have had to attend an unexpected emergency meeting. In this case, Strategy Three – **Murder with a borrowed knife** from Book One – *Tame the Tiger: Negotiating from a position of power* is being applied. This is where the company uses someone of a lower level to ask the difficult questions and conduct the negotiation.

These contacts host a dinner for you, but the restaurant is not nearly as elaborate as where you were taken on your first visit. To your surprise, at this dinner, they offer you a much cheaper price for your products: a price that is unacceptable. They also state that the company is only interested in distributing your meat products if they can have the distribution rights for the whole of China. You know that you should never give the distribution rights to one company for all of China, because if there is a dispute and you want to stop dealing with this company you may then lose the opportunity to sell anywhere in China. They have applied Strategy Ten because you have been placed in a position where '*you have been charmed*', then '*they gain your trust*' and '*they move against you*' by offering you unrealistic prices and only wanting to deal with you in a structure that is unacceptable.

EXAMPLE TWO
Guarding yourself against Strategy Ten

The important thing to keep in mind with Strategy Ten is that even though this strategy may be easy to perceive in one interaction, it is likely to appear again several times, and is often concealed inside Chinese hospitality. This high level of hospitality can make you feel relaxed, and therefore not envisage Strategy Ten. When joining a delegation to visit China, Western delegates are often advised to beware of the 'yes' that may mean 'no'. In the initial interaction there are ways of detecting Strategy Ten, such as when your contact asks many enquiring questions about your product. These focused questions often indicate a 'yes' they are interested. On the first visit you may be on red alert looking for Strategy Ten being played out on you, and feel pleased with yourself for detecting it. Also, when you know how Strategy Ten is applied, you are able to choose the distributors who are seriously interested in your products. In this case there were three distributors who were in different cities, those being Shanghai, Beijing and Qingdao. This is all good. However, you need to go to the next stage in the development of *guanxi*.

When visiting China for the second time, to meet with the three chosen distributors, even if they are in different cities in China it is crucial you meet all of these potential distributors and give them the same amount of time and focus. It is important to develop each relationship. However, when developing these relationships it is crucial to remain slightly distant, so you do not get consumed by hospitality. Ensure your judgement does not get clouded by your Chinese contact's willingness to host dinners and present you with gifts. When visiting the first distributor, do not make your decision even if you feel you trust them and can comfortably work with them. Continue on to the next meetings, giving them an equal amount of time. Do not return to the first distributor after meeting with the other two, because this displays that you have chosen the first one. This return visit will set up the framework for Strategy Ten to be played out on you.

It is advisable when looking for a distributor in China to choose three or, at the very least, two distributors. This is a risk management strategy in China, because you need to have different distributors across China. If something happens with one then you have at least one other to continue to market your products. It is not a good idea to give any distributor exclusive rights to your product, because if this distributor does not continue to market your product you may lose all of your customers across the whole of China.

When you feel relaxed and comfortable this is a time to watch out for Strategy Ten being used on you. In this case, when Strategy Ten was applied by the company in Shanghai, if the same amount of time and effort had been used with the distributors in Beijing and Qingdao, there would have been a back-up plan. Also, this third visit to the company in Shanghai allowed the company to predict that their Western visitor had chosen them as their distributor, which then gave them the opportunity to apply Strategy Ten.

Key Points when Strategy Ten is used against you

- In Chinese communication 'yes' can mean 'no'.
- A risk management strategy is to deal with more than one distributor.
- Only make the final choice about who you want to deal with when you have conducted all meetings with potential distributors.

EXAMPLE THREE
Enacting Strategy Ten

The most likely question from a potential Chinese investor who is looking to invest in your business in your country is *'What is the return on my investment?'* In many investment projects this question may be answered easily, but there are some investments where this is a difficult question to answer. When the answer to this question is unclear because of the nature of the industry, Strategy Ten is a good strategy to apply to help you gain your potential investor's trust prior to getting to the difficult conversations. One industry sector where it is difficult to answer this question is the retirement industry. This is because the return on investment is predicated only when residents leave the village and their unit is sold to a new resident, therefore, when the profit actually happens is unpredictable. To apply Strategy Ten you firstly need to build trust with your potential Chinese investor so you can explain to them why you cannot provide them with a definitive figure for the return on investment.

In this case, preparation for Strategy Ten would firstly be to conduct a site visit to the retirement village you have for sale. It is important when conducting this site visit that everything is in perfect condition, especially the grounds and the community areas. Chinese culture is a group culture, and it is appealing for them to see there are group activities. Converse with your potential Chinese investors by asking them about their country, which demonstrates you have interest in them beyond business. Show your respect for China's global economic progress. This will make them happy, as Chinese people are very proud of their country. If your potential Chinese investors do not speak English make sure you use an experienced interpreter. This means using an interpreter who is familiar with the vocabulary and linguistic nuisances in the retirement industry. When using an interpreter this rule applies for any industry, because just speaking Chinese does not make you an expert in the vocabulary of an industry sector.

After taking your potential Chinese investors on a site visit it is a good idea to spend the time, money and effort to take them to a reputable restaurant. Chinese people are likely to be entertained by good food. Keep the discussions at the dinner informal, and do not discuss the topic of return on investment until the end of the dinner, and even then only discuss this briefly. Propose a meeting the next morning at your office, when you will tell them about your connections with government and council. Knowing that you have government connections is likely to provide your potential

Chinese investors with a solid level of security. For this third meeting in your office, it is crucial you are well prepared and therefore have all of the financials documented so they are easy to understand. You can show the past performance of the retirement village demonstrating where profit has occurred. Have documents translated into Chinese, because even if your potential investors speak English this level of effort will demonstrate respect for their language and culture. Locating investments that are different – as a retirement village investment is – appeals to Chinese people because this makes them feel special. However, there will still be the question *'What is the return on investment?'*

Because of the nature of this industry there is no exact answer, so at this point you can tell your potential Chinese investors that the profit figure is unpredictable. It is likely that through your generous hospitality and the developing of *gaunxi*, this answer will be accepted, as at this point your potential Chinese investors will probably trust you enough to want to deal with you. In this situation you have *'charmed your potential Chinese investors'* and *'gained their trust'*, so you have solid ground to answer a confronting question where your answer will be unclear. If the preparation was not made and Strategy Ten was not applied, then you may lose their interest in the initial stage of contact.

Negotiating in a Western Environment

EXAMPLE FOUR
Enacting Strategy Ten

Strategy Ten can be used in a Western business environment if you have to lay-off staff. This can be a very difficult task, and is often an uncomfortable situation. If this task is conducted in a non-sensitive way it can severely damage the reputation of your business. The damage can manifest from a disgruntled ex-employee who may spread negative comments about your business. This action is likely to deter future employees or future clients from working with you. In order to enact Strategy Ten, when you retrench an employee it is crucial that this is conducted in a manner which makes the person feel positive about themselves. '*You ingratiate yourself with them*' so that '*you can gain their trust*'.

The most appropriate way to address this situation is to treat the employee with a high level of respect, by explaining exactly why they are being retrenched. Often the reason for this action is beyond the control of the company, such as an economic downturn resulting in the company no longer being able to afford the employee. If this is the case then make them aware that this change in structure is not due to the employee's performance. During this difficult discussion it is a good idea to provide them with a solid reference. Depending on the company's budget, you may want to offer them some career development with a reputable consultancy firm. If the employee leaves the company on good terms and talks about the company in a positive way, this can only be positive for the future reputation of your company.

In this situation using Strategy Ten is a good way of upholding your company's reputation while you have to deliver some disappointing news.

Key Points when using Strategy Ten

- When enacting Strategy Ten spend the time required to build the *guanxi*.
- Building trust will allow you to address difficult conversations.
- When retrenching staff always be mindful of the reputation of your company.

Sacrifice the plum tree to preserve the peach tree means *"take a small loss for a large gain"*

There are circumstances in which you must sacrifice short-term objectives in order to achieve the long-term goal. This is the scapegoat strategy, whereby someone suffers the consequences so that others do not.

*D*uring the Warring States period (475–221 BC), Tian Ji, who was a general of the Kingdom Qi, often gambled with the king of Qi through a series of three-horse races. Tian Ji and the king each had three horses. The idea was, in a descending order, the horses with the fastest time would race first. The winner of this competition was the man with the horse that won most races. Prior to applying Strategy Eleven – **Sacrifice the plum tree to preserve the peach tree,** the sequence was Tian Ji's fastest horse raced the king's fastest horse, and so on in the subsequent races. Without the application of Strategy Eleven, every time they had this competition Tian Ji lost.

Tian Ji's friend Sun Bin had been analysing this situation and saw Tian Ji's disappointment, because he was never able to win the competition. So Sun Bin advised Tian Ji to apply Strategy Eleven. Tian Ji applied Strategy Eleven by racing his third, and slowest, horse against the King of Qi's fastest horse in the first race. Tian Ji lost the first race because the strategy was to '*sacrifice short-term objectives in order to achieve the long-term goal*'. Then, for the second race, Tian Ji raced his fastest horse against the king's second fastest horse and he won the race. For the third race, Tian Ji raced his second best horse against the king's slowest horse. Tian Ji won the third race. Tian Ji sacrificed his worst horse in the first race in order to ensure a victorious win in the following two races. He '*sacrificed short-term objectives in order to achieve the long-term goal*'.

Strategy Eleven is applied when you accept small losses in order to make a greater gain. To successfully use Strategy Eleven you need to be confident you will ultimately emerge as the winner, and then minor losses become acceptable.

Negotiating with Chinese People

EXAMPLE ONE
Strategy Eleven in action (against you)

Quite often when delegations visit China from Western countries they are industry-focused and operate as a group. A delegation may consist of early childhood education providers who want to market their training courses to China for their Chinese early childhood workers. Generally, approximately ten of these Western companies travel to

China together. This style of travelling gives these Western businesses support, plus opportunities for collaboration and discussion while they are visiting China, because for most people this is still a foreign country.

It is likely that the businesses on the trip to China will be of different sizes, and therefore their capacity to deliver requests for Chinese companies will vary. For reasons such as more staff and substantial infrastructure, the larger companies will probably have the capacity to deliver the immediate and larger requests of Chinese companies. Such requests may be the development of a tailored early childhood training program, or to send Western staff to China to conduct staff training at short notice. The smaller early childhood education providers may only be able to deliver smaller, less demanding projects.

On a delegation where there are ten businesses from the same industry that are of different sizes, Strategy Eleven can easily be applied. The process of the application of Strategy Eleven is that the Chinese company will initially deal with Western businesses of a smaller size. This is because the Chinese company is aware these smaller businesses will only have the infrastructure to deliver on small projects, as they have fewer resources than the larger companies. When Strategy Eleven is applied, even though the Chinese company will deal with the smaller companies, they have no real intention to continue business dealings with them in the long-term. Once the Chinese company has learnt about the early childhood education industry on these small projects, they will then approach the larger companies. These larger Western companies have the capacity the Chinese company requires to operate successfully on a large scale. In this situation, when Strategy Eleven is applied, the smaller company is the *'short-term objective'* and the *'long-term goal'* is the larger Western company.

Strategy Eleven can appear very similar to Strategy Eight – **Openly repair the walkway, secretly march to Chen Cang.** However, Strategy Eight is about pretending you are going to do one thing while actually doing another, whereas with Strategy Eleven you make use of the resources from one thing, before dispensing with them in favour of a better, more 'fruitful' option.

Example One
Guarding yourself against Strategy Eleven

If you are a small Western company who is dealing with a large Chinese company, you may be the perfect candidate for Strategy Eleven to be employed. This is because you are unlikely to be able to meet the larger project requirements of the Chinese company. Therefore, you are viewed as a company who can only deliver on short-term projects, and it is inevitable you will be the business who is sacrificed for the *'long-term goal'*, which is a larger Western company. If you are aware of your business capacity, and that there is a strong possibility Strategy Eleven will be used on you, you do not have to see this as a negative experience, but rather, as a positive one. You can gain a positive experience from this situation by learning about conducting business with a Chinese company when you are the one who is '*sacrificed*'.

While on this learning curve guard yourself against the outcome of Strategy Eleven by dealing with three different Chinese companies, as opposed to one large Chinese company. A good mix of Chinese companies to deal with may be two small companies and one larger one. In this situation, if you are aware Strategy Eleven will be applied, when you are being '*sacrificed*' for the '*long-term goal*', you will still have two other Chinese companies with whom you can continue to conduct business. It is beneficial if the two other Chinese companies are of a comparable size to your company; these Chinese companies are likely to require the delivery of projects you can sustain in the long-term. Strategy Eleven is generally applied by a Chinese company to a much smaller Western company than them, where the Western company is only ever able to deliver on smaller, more short-term projects.

It is important that you know the capacity of your company, so that you are not deluded as to what you can actually deliver. The key is to be aware that you may have Strategy Eleven used on you and that you have thoroughly prepared yourself. Often, during a group business trip, the organisers of the trip provide a business matching structure. Part of business matching is matching according to size. However, it is often the case that smaller Western companies are matched with larger Chinese companies. This then places Western companies in the position of having Strategy Eleven used on them.

EXAMPLE TWO
Strategy Eleven in action (against you)

Strategy Eleven is used by Chinese business people on Western business people by giving away small things in the hope of achieving a larger goal. A scenario may be a Western company that is planning to import plain white T-shirts from China. This Western company has a factory in their own country. Their business is putting embroidered logos and advertising onto their T-shirts and most of their clients are conference and events organisers, requiring substantial quantities of T-shirts. The company is valued because they are able to handle the quantities involved, and also for the high quality of their T-shirts and embroidery.

They are looking for a supplier in China because operational costs in their own country have increased. Their objective is to locate a supplier in China to purchase plain white T-shirts, and they would continue to do the embroidery in their own country. However, the alternative could be to have the embroidery done in China, as this would substantially reduce costs.

This Western company plans to visit three factories in the Guangzhou area in Guangdong Province, China. The factories have been recommended by their home country government office, and despite having been checked for credibility, they know little about these factories. One of the factories appears to be extremely generous, by giving the Western company five T-shirts with sample embroidery logos. The other two factories do not present samples despite also having the facility to carry out the embroidery.

The factory that has given away the samples has conducted preliminary research on the Western company, and is aware of the high costs the Western company is facing. Knowledge of this information gives the Chinese factory enough information to successfully apply Strategy Eleven. By applying Strategy Eleven, they *'sacrificed short-term objectives'* that are the samples *'to achieve long-term goals'*, which is to secure the contract to supply the embroidery work, as well as supplying the T-shirts.

If they achieve their *'long-term goal'* they will have a large contract from a reputable Western company, and this will not only give them good revenue, it will also give them credibility. All of the three factories' prices are good, but the company that has shown them the embroidery samples is an attractive option. It is very easy to be enticed by the factory that shows their work and also gives what seems like a substantial gift. By letting the incentive place this factory at the top of the list of potential suppliers the Western company has not left time to fully explore the other two factories as possible suppliers. If factory choices are made purely by the samples they receive in the initial meeting, the Western company places themselves at risk, because they cannot be sure that the quality of embroidery they saw with the samples is what they will actually get in the final product. There is also the question of continued quality, because even if the first batch of T-shirts with embroidery is of high quality, it is difficult to provide ongoing quality control. The most effective way to achieve full quality control is to position a quality assurance person in China to check the stock, but this is very costly.

Even though giving the entire contract to the Chinese factory that was generous with their samples appears to be an excellent decision, there are risks involved. On making this decision it is easy for the Western company to be captured by the attractiveness of a *'short-term objective'*

EXAMPLE TWO
Guarding yourself against Strategy Eleven

To guard themselves against being enticed by the application of Strategy Eleven, the Western company needs to treat all three factories they visit equally. The factory that is generous with their samples may not be the best choice. This factory applied Strategy Eleven, and therefore had a larger plan in mind. When deciding which factory to import from, it is wise to choose at least two factories.

Once the Western company has started purchasing from two different sources, a good business strategy is to inform each factory that they are not the only company in China that they are purchasing goods from. This will alert these Chinese businesses that they have competition, meaning that they may be reluctant to raise the prices or reduce the quality. Additionally, it is safer to commence buying T-shirts only, as opposed to purchasing the embroidery work as well. After several shipments of T-shirts, quality and customer service can be assessed prior to entering the next stage, which is purchasing the embroidery work as well.

When the Western company met with these factories, one of the Chinese businesses applied Strategy Eleven, and so it is crucial to understand that the generosity of giving away these samples has an underlying strategy. The objective of Strategy Eleven is for this Western company to buy both the T-shirts and the embroidery work from the Chinese factory. It is important when Strategy Eleven is applied to be careful not to make hasty decisions, as the consequences can be costly.

If the Western company does eventually decide to give the embroidery work to the Chinese factories, they will need to periodically visit the factories to keep the *guanxi* strong, and to discuss any production, freight and cost issues. Most of the time the only way to sort out these issues is to visit the Chinese factories and conduct face-to-face meetings. When visiting a Chinese factory to discuss these issues it is common for the Chinese factory to apply Strategy Six– **Make a noise in the east and attack in the west,** from Book One – *Tame the Tiger: Negotiating from a position of power.* Strategy Six is used to take you away from the main point of conversation, and this diversion can cause a loss of focus from the original intention of the meeting. In this case, it may mean the Western company loses the opportunity to discuss pricing or other important issues, because they have been strategically taken away from the main point. When meeting with the Chinese factories, it is important to be clear about the objective of the meeting and to be mindful of keeping the conversation on track.

Key Points when Strategy Eleven is used against you

- Understand your capacity because if you are a small company you may be sacrificed for a larger company.
- Manage risk by working with more than one Chinese company.
- It is likely Strategy Eleven is in action against you if you are given a generous number of free samples.

EXAMPLE THREE
Enacting Strategy Eleven

An excellent way to enter the Chinese market is to organise a stand at an exhibition. Most days of the year there are numerous exhibitions in China where you can display specific products. It only takes a quick search on the internet and you will find many locations for different exhibitions. If you are a wine exporter who plans to export your wine to China you will be amazed at the amount of food and beverage exhibitions across China. Before making the financial commitment to operating a stand to exhibit your wine, it is important to understand that wine is a highly competitive product, as there are many companies globally already exporting wine to China. As wine is such a competitive product in China, it would be beneficial for a wine exporter to organise a stand at an exhibition in one of the second- or third-tier cities, such as Qingdao or Xi'an. As these cities are smaller than Chinese cities like Shanghai, Beijing and Guangzhou, there are likely to be fewer wine exporters going to these areas, therefore is easier to apply

Strategy Eleven. It is more difficult to effectively achieve all the aims of Strategy Eleven when the market is saturated with people selling a similar product, because people become more aware Strategy Eleven is in action. Therefore you may '*sacrifice short-term objectives*', and still find it difficult to '*achieve your long-term goals*'.

At an exhibition, when planning to apply Strategy Eleven, it is important to decide what you are going to give away and predict what you will receive in return. So what '*short-term objectives*' are you going to '*sacrifice*' in order for you to '*achieve your long-term goal*'? At an exhibition, the plan is to have many Chinese wine distributors walking past your stand. A way of applying Strategy Eleven is to have an attractive bowl on your front table and collect as many business cards as you can. At the end of the day draw eight business cards, because eight is a lucky number in Chinese culture, and this will demonstrate you understand the culture. The prizes will be bottles of your premium wines. In this way, you have given away the wine, which is your '*short-term objective*', to collect business cards from potential contacts in China, which is your '*long-term goal*'.

Another way of applying Strategy Eleven at an exhibition is to listen and gain information that indicates who are the most influential people visiting your stand. These people are likely to be interested in buying your wine, as they are most likely visiting the exhibition specifically to look for new products. For Strategy Eleven to be applied, you focus your attention on these key people and individually invite them out to dinner. Chinese business people feel more comfortable discussing business over a meal. In fact, most deals in China are conducted over banquets. Take some of your high-quality wine to the dinner to share with your guests. Before you leave the restaurant organise another meeting with your guests while you are still in China. This meeting is preferably at their office, and will give you a feel for their business environment. In this scenario you have applied Strategy Eleven by hosting your influential contacts at a dinner, as well as sharing some of your wine with them. These are all '*sacrifices*' for you to give away, so you '*achieve your long-term goal*'.

If this has been successful and you have conducted deals with the Chinese distributor or distributors, you can once again apply Strategy Eleven. In this scenario, if you are working with more than one distributor, you will need to decide which distributor is worth the reapplication of Strategy Eleven. To encourage your Chinese distributor to be proactive when marketing your wine it is a good idea to spend the time and money and fund their travelling expenses in order for them to visit you in your country. Applying Strategy Eleven in this way will give the distributor a clearer picture of your physical environment, and a better understanding of your product and its origin. As a result of their visit their product knowledge will be much higher, which will help them sell more of your product in China. In this scenario, the sacrifice of the '*short-term objectives*' is using the resources for your distributor to visit you. The Chinese wine distributor then becomes more knowledgeable about your wine, which in turn generates more sales in China, which is your '*long-term goal*'.

Negotiating in a Western Environment

EXAMPLE FOUR
Enacting Strategy Eleven

Strategy Eleven can be applied when the goal is to gain more customers. Strategy Eleven is a good strategy to use if you are in a business such as a gymnasium, because in this kind of business Strategy Eleven can be successfully used in several ways. To apply Strategy Eleven, the gymnasium can offer a one-week free trial. This sacrifice of the offer of a one-week free trial is the '*short-term objective*', which is to convert these people who use the one-week free trial into members, which is the '*long-term goal*'. The idea is that by the end of the one-week free trial, these people will feel it is worthwhile entering a membership contract. Often, the best value for money most gymnasiums offer are one-year memberships, therefore, by using Strategy Eleven they gain new customers signing up for one-year memberships.

Another way a gymnasium can use Strategy Eleven is to entice its existing members to refer new members. In this scenario existing members may be offered a one-month free membership if they refer a person to buy a one-year membership. The one-month free membership is the '*short-term objective*', which is to gain more members to achieve the '*long-term goal*'.

Key Points when using Strategy Eleven
- If your product is competitive in China it is better to market it to one of the second or third-tier cities, as opposed to the first-tier cities.
- Work out what you can give away in order to get a larger return.
- You can apply Strategy Eleven multiple times to the same product.

Seize the opportunity to lead a sheep away means "take advantage of every opportunity"

While carrying out your plans, be flexible enough to take advantage of any opportunity that presents itself, however small, and avail yourself of any profit, however slight.

*D*uring the final days of the Yuan dynasty there was a large rebellion throughout the empire. After much fighting to determine who would found a new dynasty, the battle was narrowed down to two contenders, Chu Yuanchang and Chen Yifu. In order to settle this conflict and determine who would found the new dynasty they transported their armies to Poyang Lake, where the battle between the two armies took place. Chen Yifu had a strong advantage in this battle, because he had more troops and much larger, sturdier ships. Chen Yifu used his ships to line up side-by-side along the entire length of the lake, and then joined the ships with iron chains in order to create a barrier. Even though Chu Yuanchang knew he was at a disadvantage he still tried to attack Chen Yifu's ships, but it was impossible for him to break through this barrier. On the second day of the battle there was a strong wind blowing, and Chu Yuanchang used this to his advantage by applying Strategy Twelve – **Seize the opportunity to lead a sheep away.** Chu Yuanchang *'took advantage of this opportunity'* and launched fireboats against Chen Yifu's barrier. The wind was blowing in the right direction to ignite Chen Yifu's ships, which sent his troops into a state of chaos. Chen Yifu's troops were so preoccupied with trying to protect their ships against the wind and fire that they were defeated by Chu Yuanchang's troops.

When Strategy Twelve is used, the strategist takes advantage of any opportunity that presents itself. The opportunity may only be small, but in the eyes of the strategist it is still an opportunity and therefore should not be ignored. Strategy Twelve may seem similar to Strategy Five – **Loot a burning house,** which is in Book One – *Tame the Tiger: Negotiating from a position of power.* The difference is that Strategy Five is used when there is an opportunity to be found inside a crisis, whereas in Strategy Twelve you take advantage of any opportunity, as Chu Yuanchang did when the wind changed direction. Strategy Twelve may also look like Strategy Nine – **Watching the fire on the opposite shore**. Unlike Strategy Twelve, Strategy Nine is in action when you wait patiently for a situation to unfold before making a move, whereas Strategy Twelve is about taking advantage of any opportunity at any given moment.

Negotiating with Chinese People

EXAMPLE ONE
Strategy Twelve in action (against you)

Whether Chinese people are communicating in a business or personal situation, or a formal or informal communication structure, they are usually looking for opportunities. The environment for opportunism to take place is irrelevant. Business opportunities can be found in social or business settings. This means Chinese people are constantly applying Strategy Twelve. It is of no consequence whether the opportunity is small or large, as a small opportunity can be seen as having the capacity to grow into something large. The potential opportunity should not be ignored, because for Chinese people the idea is to *'be flexible enough to take advantage of any opportunity that presents itself, however 'small'.*

As China's middle-class population continues to grow, more Chinese tourists are choosing to travel in Western countries, to enjoy the well-known tourist attractions and experience other cultures. It is common for Chinese tourists to join a tour group, as most Chinese people prefer their trip to be fully organised. As Western wine has gained strong momentum in China, it is popular for Chinese tour groups to visit wineries when touring Western countries. Visiting wineries gives Chinese tourists a real-life experience of the vineyard environment, because they see first-hand where the grapes are grown and where the wine is made.

Western tourists generally perceive a holiday as a rest, and therefore do their best not to let their work enter into their holiday activities. On the other hand, for Chinese tourists, holiday time and work time all blend into one, and they see applying Strategy Twelve in the context of seeking business opportunities to be normal activity during a holiday. This is a key difference between how Chinese people and Western people perceive work and leisure, because even as tourists Chinese people are continually looking for business opportunities. They are constantly applying Strategy Twelve.

In a scenario where a Chinese person visits a winery when on tour in a Western country, if they are impressed with the quality of the wine, they may see an opportunity to export the wine to China to sell to Chinese consumers. Despite the Chinese person's knowledge of wine being limited they will still pursue this business opportunity and apply Strategy Twelve. When Strategy Twelve is applied, the opportunity overrides the experience and knowledge of the product. In fact, having experience of the product is often irrelevant in order for the Chinese person to move towards conducting a business deal. Western people find this concept strange, because in Western culture it is considered vital to understand the product and the market before engaging in any business discussion.

It is unlikely that wineries who have opened their doors to Chinese tour groups would expect to be approached by Chinese tourists regarding the possibility of exporting their wine to China. When Strategy Twelve is applied and the Chinese tourist is '*taking advantage of any opportunity that presents itself*, the Western person is unlikely to be prepared for this situation. There is then a risk of setting up a business deal where the Western person sells the product too cheaply. In Chinese culture Strategy Twelve is constantly in action, and it is often difficult to predict when this will happen. To *'take advantage of any opportunity'*, Chinese people are ready to step out of what they are doing and change direction so they can fully explore the opportunity. In the scenario of visiting a Western winery, the Chinese tourist is able to quickly adapt to a business opportunity discussion and step out of being a tourist.

EXAMPLE ONE
Guarding yourself against Strategy Twelve

As Strategy Twelve is in action most of the time it is very easy not to be well-prepared when it is used on you. A safe way to operate is to acquire the mindset that Strategy Twelve is always in action when communicating with Chinese people. This does not mean constantly being on high alert, it simply means having the knowledge that Strategy Twelve exists. The environment in which you communicate is irrelevant, because it does not matter if you are communicating in a business or social situation. Whatever the circumstances, it is highly likely Strategy Twelve will be played out.

In the example of the winery, it is important to firstly understand Chinese people do not separate their business life from their personal life. Even when on holiday most Chinese people are always looking for opportunities. For the winery to guard themselves against Strategy Twelve, the winery staff who are greeting the Chinese tourists need to be prepared for questions relating to business dealings from the Chinese tourists.

If the winery is not interested in exporting their wine to China it is important they have an appropriate answer prepared. On the other hand, this may be a great opportunity for the winery, if they are interested in exporting their wine. If they are interested in exporting their wine to China they need to have prices ready, and be prepared to discuss this opportunity. In the situation where a Chinese tour group visits the winery it is a good idea for the winery to allocate specific staff to look after any Chinese person who approaches the winery about the exporting of the wine. If staff are not specifically allocated for these business questions, the winery will find that the Chinese person who wants to discuss business will consume all of the staff's time. This may result in the rest of the Chinese tour group not getting the service they have paid for. The winery should keep in mind when entertaining Chinese tourists that there will probably be at least one person in the group who wants to discuss a business deal with them. The person assigned to discussing such business needs to have prices, export information and any other issues organised relating to the potential business deal prepared. If there is no preparation for such questions from a member of the tour group who is interested in proposing a business deal, the winery may offer a less than appropriate price, which is likely to result in dissatisfaction for the winery.

Example Two
Strategy Twelve in action (against you)

At any time you are travelling to China to market your product you are likely to have Strategy Twelve played out on you. The main reason for Strategy Twelve to be the most likely strategy used is because most Chinese people are generally opportunistic, and the application of Strategy Twelve's main focus is to seek out new opportunities. When you visit China and you are meeting with your contacts to show them what you have to offer you may be questioned about other possible opportunities. Most of the time Western business people are not prepared for these peripheral questions, because it is the Western way to focus on their specific product, which is what they have expertise in. When your Chinese contacts meet with you, they are generally seeking more than the product you are selling, because they will be looking to '*take advantage of any opportunity that presents itself.* They are likely to ask you about possible opportunities that relate indirectly to your product.

You may be marketing your wine to China, and while discussing your wine with your Chinese contacts they may ask you if you know of any wineries for sale in your country because they are looking for investment opportunities. Or they may ask if you have contacts who want to export olives or meat products. Most of the time when Strategy Twelve is used on you the questioning of opportunities will have a connection to your product. However, they may ask about an opportunity which is totally unrelated. The risk here is that you may know nothing about other opportunities, and therefore do not know how to answer their questions. Strategy Twelve may look like Strategy Six – **Make a Noise in the East and attack in the West** from Book One – *Tame the Tiger: Negotiating from a position of power*. However, Strategy Six is about creating diversions, whereas Strategy Twelve is about looking at the bigger picture.

In most cases Western business people become experts in a particular field of knowledge, and then they learn business skills for their area of expertise in order to run a successful business. Chinese business people, on the other hand, learn business and negotiation skills, and perceive these skills as useful for any business environment, and therefore they do not see that they have to be an expert in any particular area to operate a business. It is for this reason that we see Chinese business people operating several businesses, and these businesses can be unrelated. They can therefore ask you questions that are not relevant to your area of expertise. Chinese people will often seek out opportunities they perceive will be popular in China.

You may be marketing childcare services, however your Chinese contact may ask you about aged care, and you are unlikely to be prepared for questions in an area in which you have limited experience. The reason you have been asked this question is because this sector has gained popularity in China.

Example Two
Guarding yourself against Strategy Twelve

When Strategy Twelve is used on you and you are faced with these questions it is important that you reply with an answer. You may be working in the childcare industry, and therefore have no connections with aged care, and your Chinese contact is asking you about aged care. However, it is likely you know someone who is involved in aged care. It is important to use your networks to answer their questions. You can generally predict that most questions about business opportunities will be related to popular sectors in China. Therefore, to address Strategy Twelve, you can research what is popular in China and then try to have some answers to the questions you may be asked. Even if your Chinese contact does not appear to be interested in your product, if you try to answer their questions, this is an excellent way of building *guanxi*. Often, it is the quality of the *guanxi* which wins you deals, as opposed to the quality of your product.

Key Points when Strategy Twelve is used against you

- Chinese business people will seek an opportunity regardless of the size of the opportunity.
- In Chinese culture there are no divisions between holidays and exploring business opportunities.
- Be prepared to be questioned about business opportunities that are not related to your business.

Example Three
Enacting Strategy Twelve

When you meet a Chinese business person for the first time, from their perspective it will not seem strange that you are applying Strategy Twelve, which is to '*be flexible enough to take advantage of any opportunity that presents itself*. If you are introduced to a Chinese business person who you feel has no knowledge of your core business, unlike in a Western business environment, this does not indicate there are no opportunities for you.

If you are exporting beef and you meet a Chinese business person who is connected with childcare products, you can apply Strategy Twelve by asking them if they have any connections in the beef industry. Being connected with diverse groups of people is a key aspect of Chinese business culture. Therefore, your contact is likely to have connections in the beef industry, even though their business is in childcare products. The benefit of applying Strategy Twelve is that you will be able to see Chinese business people as being part of a wide circle of Chinese businesses, and then benefit from these many connections.

Applying Strategy Twelve means that you are not limited to talking with people who are in a similar business to you. This widening of your vision means you will be able to meet Chinese business people from many sectors and you are therefore not limited to meeting people connected only with your product. Even though they have no connection with your product, they are likely to be able to connect you with their Chinese contacts who are interested in your product. In your initial meetings, it is irrelevant if the Chinese business person has no direct interest in your product, because when you apply Strategy Twelve you are taking control of the situation by being proactive and enquiring about who they know that may be interested in meeting with you.

Generally, this control and proactivity is well received by Chinese business people. Applying Strategy Twelve will not only widen your opportunities, it will also give you the reputation of being someone who Chinese business people want to work with.

Negotiating in a Western Environment

EXAMPLE FOUR
Enacting Strategy Twelve

Attending networking events in Western business environments is a perfect place to enact Strategy Twelve. Applying Strategy Twelve not only provides you with more opportunities, it also gives you a direct reason to attend the networking function. To use Strategy Twelve at a networking event means you will '*be flexible enough to take advantage of any opportunities that presents itself*'.

When applying Strategy Twelve, even if the person with whom you are talking seems like they have no connection with your business, it is crucial to look beyond what someone's business card says, as they may have useful contacts.

Strategy Twelve is about seeing possibilities and seeking opportunities. People you meet at a networking function may not be directly connected with your industry. However, it is possible they have worked in your business sector in the past, and therefore know people they can introduce you to. Generally, people like to talk about themselves, so to develop a good communication connection, even when the people you meet ask you about your background, do not spend too much time talking about yourself. Instead, ask questions about them. By doing this you will not only make them feel comfortable, you will also gain a lot of information about them and they may be able to connect you with the appropriate people in your industry.

When applying Strategy Twelve it is important to place yourself in many different business-networking environments, as opposed to limiting yourself to the business sector with which you are most familiar. By doing this you are widening your circle of business contacts and, in turn, your opportunities.

Key Points when using Strategy Twelve

- The application of Strategy Twelve is well respected by Chinese business people.
- If someone has no connection with your business, this does not mean they cannot introduce you to opportunities.
- Perceive every person you meet at a networking function as a road to an opportunity.

Your Next Steps

Having just finished reading *Deceive the Dragon*, here are some suggestions for your next steps:

- Now I can plan my approach when I am negotiating in any situation.
- The 36 Strategies will help me when communicating with Chinese people.
- I will share this knowledge with my colleagues.
- I want to read *The Dao of Negotiation* series. I'll find them at **www.leoniemckeon.com**
- I will contact Leonie to:
  - Help me think completely differently about my business development challenges.
  - Deliver a presentation for my next conference or other event.
  - Deliver 36 Strategies workshops to my team.
- Because **Pronounce Mandarin - The Easy Way** is perfect for beginners, I will learn how to correctly pronounce Chinese names and some useful Mandarin Chinese words and phrases via **www.pronouncemandarin.com**

Go to **www.leoniemckeon.com** for more information about the 36 Strategies. Leonie has several informative videos and blogs to help you further your understanding of how to negotiate in any business environment.

WHAT PEOPLE SAY ABOUT WORKING WITH LEONIE MCKEON

BEC HARDY WINES

"I can't tell you how much you have given our family, and me personally, through your insights about the 36 Chinese Strategies. Understanding how the 36 Chinese Strategies are applied in Chinese business culture was the lightbulb moment which has led to such revenue growth, opportunities and personal growth. This has been one of the great, exciting professional and personal journeys and achievements of my life. Thanks again."

Richard Dolan, Joint Managing Director

HATCH, Western Australia

"Anyone who has the pleasure of having dealings with China and the Chinese will find Leonie's 36 Chinese Strategies workshops invaluable. The workshops were eye-opening and had the right amount of humour and personal stories to more than keep our attention."

Denis Pesci, PDG Hub Director, Western Australia

Fletcher Building

"From a personal perspective, Leonie was instrumental to our Chinese cultural program developed for the Super Retail Group. The target audience for the workshop was our Management and Leaders from Logistics, Marketing and Category. In organising the program for the team, I found Leonie incredibly resourceful, totally understood the brief and built value-add to the program. Often you don't know what you don't know so great to have a Subject Matter Expert to guide and shape a very successful program."

Shirley Brown, Capability Development Manager –
Australian Distribution

Australian American Fulbright Commission

"The Art of Negotiation – 36 Strategies derived from 'The Art of War' workshop delivered by Leonie at the Australian Institute of Company Directors (AICD) challenged conventional thinking."

Peter de Cure, Chairman, Australian American Fulbright
Commission

Kmart

"The training that Leonie provided to our team was excellent. The program was practical, delivered with context, and opened the team members' minds to learning more about how to do better business in China. I have no doubt that what we have learned will be applied and will provide great outcomes for our business. Leonie has also provided a great personal development opportunity for members of our team."

Matthew Webber, International Supply Chain Manager

The Dao of Negotiation
The Path between Eastern Strategies and Western Minds

		Strategy Number
Book One – *Tame the Tiger*	Advantageous Strategies	1, 2, 3, 4, 5, 6
Book Two – *Deceive the Dragon*	Opportunistic Strategies	7, 8, 9, 10, 11, 12,
Book Three – *Lure the Tiger*	Strategies for Attack	13, 14, 15, 16, 17, 18
Book Four – *Bewilder the Dragon*	Confusion Strategies	19, 20, 21, 22, 23, 24
Book Five – *Endure the Tiger*	Strategies for Gaining Ground	25, 26, 27, 28, 29, 30
Book Six – *Flee the Dragon*	Strategies for Desperate Situations	31, 32, 33, 34, 35, 36

The Dao of Negotiation:
The Path between Eastern Strategies
and Western Minds

by Leonie McKeon

More Control, More Success, More Wins!

Based on *The Art of War*, *The Dao of Negotiation* series unmask the 36 Strategies used in Chinese culture and business.

This incredible series of 6 books provide invaluable tips for any business person looking to improve their overall negotiation skills, as well as become better at negotiating with Chinese People.

Discover how you can use this ancient wisdom for more business success.

www.leoniemckeon.com